MW01227173

James A. Quick

and His House in Gaylord

Kenneth Lingaur

Lingaur Preservation LLC
Clare, Michigan
2018

James A. Quick and His House in Gaylord

Copyright © 2018 by Kenneth Lingaur

No part of this book may be reproduced in any manner, except with the written permission of Kenneth Lingaur.

Lingaur Preservation LLC
Clare, Michigan
www.lingaurpreservation.com
Printed in the U.S.A.

ISBN-13: 978-1-7322263-1-9
ISBN-10: 1-7322263-1-8

Cover design by Heather Todd

To my mother,
Eunice Lingaur
we share a love of history.

Table of Contents

Acknowledgements

First, I would like to thank Gary Scott, the owner of the James A. Quick House. He took a chance at hiring me, a man with little experience, to write a National Register of Historic Places Nomination and a Federal Historic Tax Credit application for this property. Thank you for your faith in me.

Phil Alexander from the Otsego County Historical Society was a great help at providing historic photographs and providing content suggestions. He went above and beyond what I had hoped for.

Bob Christensen from the Michigan State Historic Preservation Office was instrumental in the final edits of the National Register of Historic Places Nomination for the Quick House. Much of the text for this book came from the nomination.

Finally, I am thankful for my wife, Sherrie, who is a constant source of encouragement and support in everything I do.

Introduction

On August 4, 2016, the house located at 120 North Center Street in Gaylord, Michigan, was officially listed on the National Register of Historic Places. The historic name given to the house is the James A. and Lottie J. (Congdon) Quick House. The house is locally significant for the reasons listed in the Significance Statement of the Nomination:

The house at 120 North Center Street is significant under national register criterion B for its association with James A. Quick. Mr. Quick was a successful businessman during the late nineteenth and early twentieth century in Gaylord. On his own and in partnership with his brother Charles Quick and another local businessman, Almon Comstock, James A. Quick was involved in a broad variety of businesses in Gaylord and the surrounding area a livery stable, general stores, and banking and he also invested in local real estate, owned and developed local property that included a hotel/boarding house building located near his house. The James A. Quick House is also significant under criterion C as one of Gaylord's most distinguished and intact Queen Anne homes.

As the author of the nomination, I decided to write a book to share this information with others. It takes the text from the National Register of Historic Places Nomination, with some edits, and tells the story of James Quick. Many of the historic photographs and newspaper clippings featured here were not included in the nomination, but are added to tell the story. Some of the historic photographs included may not be of the best quality, but I believe a bad picture is better than no picture. Enjoy learning about James A. Quick and his house in Gaylord.

James A. Quick

James A. Quick was born in Oakland County, Michigan, on October 7, 1857. He lived and worked on his father's farm until he moved to the Gaylord area in 1881, following his older brother Charles A. Quick, who moved to Gaylord in 1879.

Gaylord, which is located in the northern part of Michigan's Lower Peninsula, was rich in timber in the mid-nineteenth century. In the mid-1860s the first explorations of the area were made by timber cruisers looking for marketable timber. In 1869 Charles Brink looked to set up a lumber operation on

James Alexander Quick
Photograph from
Gaylord Illustrated, 1907
Courtesy of the Otsego
County Historical Society
Collection

the southeast corner of Otsego Lake, a few miles south of today's Gaylord, but the location proved to be too remote and the effort was abandoned. Full scale cutting of timber would have to wait until a railroad served the region.

The Jackson, Lansing and Saginaw Railroad was the first railroad line built in this area. It was built as far north as Otsego Lake in 1873. In anticipation of the railroad being built farther north, the town of Barnes was platted in 1874 by Orlando M. Barnes of Lansing. He was a leading figure in the railroad's management, serving as the company's secretary and, beginning in 1872, land commissioner. When the railroad was completed to Barnes in 1874, the place was renamed Gaylord in honor of Augustine Smith Gaylord, who then served as the railroad's attorney. Three years later, in 1877, the county seat was moved from Otsego Lake Village to Gaylord.

In 1881, the year James Quick moved to Gaylord, the town was incorporated as a village. It had a population of 400, but was experiencing a boom in growth due to the railroad connection and the line's extension north toward Mackinac, which was just beginning. James Quick purchased an eighty-acre farm just outside of Gaylord. Quick's obituary states that about two years after Charles' 1879 arrival, "in 1881 James A. Quick came to Gaylord to

Quick Brothers Livery, 1880s
Photograph from the Otsego County Historical Society Collection

engage in business with his brother, C. A. Quick, the two having arranged to establish a livery stable here. Immediately following the arrival of James A. Quick the two set to work to procure the timber and erect a suitable barn and arrange for the conduct of the livery business which they succeeded in establishing in the early part of 1883." Their livery barn was located directly across the street from the future Quick residence on North Center Street.

The obituary reports that James and Charles Quick continued their livery barn partnership for about eight years (until about 1891) and then disposed of the business while retaining ownership of the building (though the State Gazetteers list the Quick Brothers Livery through the 1895 edition). They then, the obituary states, relocated to Gould City in Mackinac County in the eastern Upper Peninsula and under the Quick Brothers name operated a "mercantile business" there for about four years, then sold that store and returned to Gaylord.

In 1896 the brothers purchased property in down-

Our Complete Stock of

Fall and Winter Goods

ARE AT YOUR DISPOSAL,

Consisting of Hats, Caps, all kinds of Rubbers. Underwear, Gloves and Mittens,

In fact everything to keep you warm and comfortable through the long winter months. Our Caps are the very latest. We are offering some exceptionally fine bargains in woolen underwear. A full line of the

CELEBRATED DOUGLASS SHOES

just arrived. We are also headquarters for Fur Overcoats. Give us a call and be convinced that we are showing the best goods in Otsego County.

'Phone 58.   QUICK BROS.

Quick Brothers Store Advertisement
Otsego County Times
January 9, 1903

Quick Brothers Store Building, circa 1920s
Northwest Corner of Main and Center Streets
Photograph Courtesy of Jan White
from the Otsego County Historical Society Collection

Quick Brothers Store, New Toledo
Photograph from the Otsego County Historical Society Collection

town Gaylord and opened a new Quick Brothers Store. The 1897 State Gazetteer is the first to list their Gaylord general store. This store was located at the northwest corner of Main and Center Streets. They also had a general store at New Toledo, later called Quick, a lumber camp located about seven miles to the east and one mile south of Gaylord. When the federal government established a post office in New Toledo in 1899 it was located in the Quick Brothers Store. The establishment of a post office required a change in the place's name since there was already a New Toledo in Michigan, and there could not be two post offices with the same name. The place acquired the name Quick, and James Quick became the first Postmaster, serving until his death.

Another business partnership of James Quick's involved his brother Charles Quick along with another Gaylord businessman, Almon B. C. Comstock. A. B. C Comstock arrived in Gaylord one year before Charles Quick in 1878. Upon his arrival he opened a hardware and tin shop. The current brick building at the northeast corner of Court and Main Streets was constructed by him after the wood frame building he operated out of was destroyed by fire. Comstock was involved in politics, being elected as the supervisor of

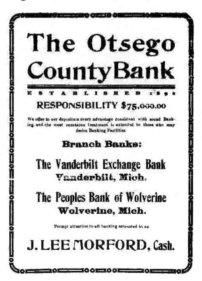

Otsego County Bank
Advertisement
Otsego County Times
December 7, 1906

[9]

Livingston Township, in which most of Gaylord was located, three times, and also served as chairman of the Otsego County Poor Board.

James and Charles Quick and A. B. C. Comstock together established Gaylord's second bank, the Otsego County Bank, in 1892. The older bank in town was the Gaylord Exchange Bank. Another bank, the Gaylord State Savings Bank, followed the next year. Although the Gaylord State Savings Bank would grow to be larger than the Otsego County Bank, the Otsego County Bank was

A. B. C. Comstock Building, circa 1920s
Northeast corner of Main and Court Streets
The Comstock Hardware store was located on the left,
The Otsego County Bank was located on the right.
Photograph from the Otsego County Historical Society Collection

still significant to the community. Advertisements for the bank in the first decade of the twentieth century publicized the bank's responsibilities at $75,000. The Gaylord State Savings Bank on the other hand had deposits of $200,000 as of 1905. By 1907 another Gaylord businessman, J. Lee Morford, also became a partner (and also was then serving as the bank's cashier). The Quicks, Comstock, and Morford also established as branches of the bank the Vanderbilt Exchange Bank at Vanderbilt, eight miles north of Gaylord, in 1905, and the Peoples Bank of Wolverine at Wolverine, ten miles north of Vanderbilt in the southwest corner of Cheboygan County, in 1906. All three banks proved to be successful. The Otsego County Bank, although sound financially, was sold to the Gaylord State Savings Bank in 1919. The Vanderbilt Exchange Bank continued into the 1950s, and the Peoples Bank of Wolverine operated until the early part of the 1910s.

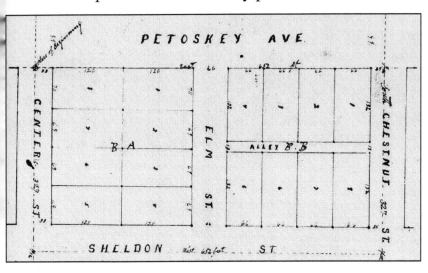

Comstock and Quick's Addition to the Village of Gaylord
Drawing from Comstock and Quick Addition Plat Map

The James Quick, Charles Quick and A. B. C. Comstock partnership was also active in the area of real estate. The most significant of their real estate activities for Gaylord itself was the platting of the Comstock and Quick Addition to the city in 1905. This sixteen-lot subdivision was bounded by Petoskey Avenue, Sheldon Street, Center Street, and the no longer existing Chestnut Street. Real estate, in general, was a major money maker for Quick. Whether solely, in partnership with his brother Charles, or in partnership with Charles and A. B. C. Comstock, James Quick profited through his real estate investments, which included over 1,300 acres of land along with numerous city lots in Gaylord, Vanderbilt, Wolverine, and also property in the "Wah Wah Soo Pleasure Resort" located along the center of the east side of Otsego Lake. It was a resort for the more well-to-do members of the Village of Gaylord.

Another of his investments was in a building located on the lot directly south of his house on North Center Street. When Quick acquired the three-story building is unclear, but several newspaper notices during 1906 and 1907 make references to it. The building is not shown on the 1898 Sanborn Map, but does appear along with Quick's House on the 1907 map. The May 4, 1906, *Otsego County Times* reported that "Workmen are just now putting the finishing touches" on the building, which Quick "has been remodeling for the past six weeks." The building was to become Mrs. Frank Mack's boarding house. The following month (June 22) the *Times* noted that Mrs. Mack's "hotel and boarding house" would be called the Delmont. Quick's building suffered a fire sometime

Delmont Hotel, in background of photograph, circa 1920
Photograph from the Otsego County Historical Society Collection

around May 1907 by which it was "partially destroyed," but was being renovated again into a rooming and boarding house as of early June (*Times,* June 7, 1907). In September 1907 Quick leased the Delmont for three years to Frank Wransky of Traverse City, "for many years connected with the Park Place hotel" there (*Times,* September 2, 1907). The Delmont Hotel continued to operate until the 1920s and was known as "the business man's hotel." The building no longer stands.

In 1902 James Quick's ill health caused him to withdraw from active business. He sold his interest in the Quick Brothers Store in 1903 to his brother Charles, who continued it until 1912, when he sold out to Leon and Harry Parmater. Quick's obituary stated that "Since 1902 Mr. Quick has not been actively engaged in any business except to interest himself in the buggy and cutter business in a small way from time to time more as a matter of occupying his attention than as a matter of real business." Quick bought out the vehicle and cutter stock from another local firm in 1906 and, according to a brief newspaper notice from July, is "making a considerable bustle for the business" (*Times,* July 20, 1906). After adding to his stock of vehicles in 1907 he moved his business from the Cook Brothers building on Main Street to the old Quick Brothers livery barn across the street from his residence on Center Street.

Despite James Quick's illness in 1902 and the comment in his

The FAMOUS
Blue Ribbon Line

Of Vehicles

Cannot be beaten anywhere.

You do not care how well I have bought them, its how cheap I will sell.
Come and see what I have, I will guarantee my prices to be cheaper than any others of the same, high grade.

James A. Quick

Cook Bros.' vacant store, Main street, Gaylord, Mich.

James A. Quick
Advertisement from
Otsego County Times
May 31, 1907

obituary about him not being actively engaged in business thereafter, he did not disengage himself from the affairs of the Gaylord community. In 1903 he was elected to a three-year term on the village council, and was re-elected to a two-year term in 1906. This was not his first experience with public office. At some prior unknown time he held the position of Livingston Township Treasurer.

As a Village Trustee, Quick served on both the Water & Light Committee and the License Committee all of his five years on the Council. He also served on the Fire Department, Rules, and Street Committees during differing years of his service. His time on the Village Council was noted for its upgrading of the village's infrastructure. Those improvements included the construction of a two-inch galvanized gas pipe with "T" connections to each lot within the village

James A. Quick
Otsego County Times
September 20, 1907

starting in 1903. In 1905, the Council passed a resolution that all new sidewalks be constructed of cement. That same year the sidewalk in front of the Quick residence was constructed. Although James Quick was not on the Street Committee that worked on the sidewalk resolution, he was on the committee the following year, 1906, when the Council voted to discontinue the Village of Gaylord's role in constructing sidewalks. Instead of directly building sidewalks, the village encouraged the construction of more sidewalks by authorizing a tax rebate of two and one half cents per square foot to any citizen who undertook the replacement or new construction of a cement sidewalk.

A major upgrade of the village's water system was the main accomplishment of the Village Council while James

Quick was a trustee. The replacement of the water storage tank took place in 1906, and new water pumps were installed and connected in January 1907. The original water storage tank was located on the lot immediately to the east of James Quick's residence. After the old water tank was removed the village authorized the sale of the lot where it was located, and James Quick obtained the lot by submitting his sealed bid.

As part of the License Committee, James Quick assisted in writing the first village ordinance restricting the sale of alcohol within the village limits. The ordinance raised the fee necessary to obtain a liquor license in the Village to $500. The State of Michigan already required a fee of $500 for a liquor license, and this additional fee would bring the total to $1,000. Permission from the state legislature was required for this provision of the ordinance, which was easily obtained. In addition, the ordinance limited the number of liquor licenses issued to businesses within the Village of Gaylord to six.

In addition to his business and political interests James Quick also devoted some of his attention to farming. Although he was not actively involved with the day-to-day activities of the farm he purchased in 1882, he was nonetheless involved in its overall operation. By the time of his death the eighty-acre farm had been expanded to one hundred and sixty acres. James' interest

> James Quick has a private toboggan slide upon which he sometimes enjoys himself. Monday he was on his barn and shoveled the snow from the "flat roof" part. He then went down a short ladder to the "leanto" part. This is where the toboggan slide begins. It ends in about a foot of slush behind the barn.

Otsego County Times
February 16, 1906

in farming also led him to serve as president of the Otsego County Agricultural Society in 1906 and 1907. The purpose of the society was to plan for and hold the annual county fair. From the *Otsego County Times* write-up of the 1906 fair, it would seem the fair was ordinary when compared to previous years. However, the paper's 1907 summary of the fair was much longer and much more enthusiastic. The paper exclaimed that it was "Bigger and Better than Ever." Quick's success with the county fair resulted in him being named to head the committee which prepared the Otsego County exhibit for the Michigan State Fair. This was a position he held in 1907 and 1908.

During his life James A. Quick was considered one of the prominent citizens of Gaylord. The *Otsego County Times* printed a special edition in September 1905 for the purpose of attracting new manufacturing industries and settlers to purchase unimproved farm lands in the area. A photograph of James along with a short bio and a photograph of his residence were featured in this edition of the paper. Two years later a small picture pamphlet, *Gaylord Illustrated*, which featured important people and buildings in Gaylord, also featured Quick and his residence.

James Quick married Lottie J. Congdon on Thanksgiving Day 1895. They had no children except for a daughter, Juliette Leona, who they adopted when she was very young. He was a member of the Gaylord Lodge of the Free & Accepted Masons, Order of the Eastern Stars, Masonic Benefit Association, Maccabees and Knights of Pythias, and the Gaylord Congregational Church. His illness in 1902 left him in a weakened state that he never fully recovered from. As a result later in life, after being ill for two weeks, he passed away from typhoid fever on September 8, 1909. He died at the age of fifty-two. He was survived by two brothers, Charles and Adrian, both of Gaylord and a sister Mrs. Mary A. Brosiur of Genesee County. He was preceded in death by a brother, Abram Quick who was killed by a cyclone in 1896. James Quick's body was taken to his former home in Oakland County for burial at the Ortonville Cemetery. His wife Lottie would later remarry to Charles Albert Horton, and they lived in Flint, Michigan (the second marriage for both of them). Lottie lived until 1937, when she died at the age of 67. She is buried in the Ortonville Cemetery next to her first husband James Quick.

The Quick House

James A. Quick House at 120 North Center Street
Photograph from Gaylord Illustrated, 1907
Courtesy of the Otsego County Historical Society Collection

A review of the local tax records suggests that James A. Quick's house at 120 North Center Street was built in 1900. The lot he built the house on was purchased jointly by him and his brother Charles in January 1890. It was not until January 1903 that James bought out Charles' interest in the property. This was the same time that James Quick sold his interest in the Quick Brothers business to his brother Charles.

James Quick lived in his house from the time of its construction until his early death at the age of fifty-two in 1909. His wife Lottie Quick took over his business activities after his death, besides the running of her Gaylord millinery store which she opened in 1906. By August 1912 she had sold her millinery business and opened a new millinery store in the Detroit area. She continued to manage the business affairs of her former husband into the 1920s. After her move to Detroit the house sat vacant for about one year. In October 1913, Dr. Harry Knapp (see

PRICES ON
MILLINERY GOODS
GREATLY
REDUCED!

On Saturday, March 17, we will place on sale a large stock of

LADIES' STREET HATS,
CHILDREN'S CAPS and
CHILDREN'S SCHOOL HATS.

We must close out these to make room for the Spring Stock. Don't fail to look in during this sale (it lasts only ten days) and see if you will not be able to find a genuine bargain.

Mrs. Lottie Quick,

OPPOSITE COURT HOUSE,   GAYLORD, MICH.

Mrs. Lottie Quick Millinery
Advertisement
Otsego County Times
March 16, 1906

page 22) purchased the house with the intent of using it for his residence and medical office. In November 1913, Dr. Knapp constructed a separate entrance for his patients on the house's south side. Dr. Knapp sold the house in March 1919 to Dr. William Housen, a local dentist (see page 24), and owned it for two years. Another dentist, Dr. Charles Saunders (see page 25), purchased the house in June 1921. Dr. Saunders lived there for forty-nine years until his death in 1970. Charles Saunders practiced dentistry in the house at the start of his ownership, but by 1936 he relocated his dental practice to an office above the Audrain Hardware Store in Gaylord. The 1968-1969 Gaylord City Directory

DAD JOKES

Why Your Family Is Avoiding You

Chuck L. Worthy

Chuckle Chums

CONTENTS

Welcome to the family fellow "Chuckle Chum!"

It appears you enjoy laughing as much as we do! Thank you for your purchase! Please follow us on our socials by going to the website below. We want to laugh with you!

Subscribe to our email list if you would like
TWO FREE DIGITAL GAG BOOKS

AND future product updates!

www.ChuckleChums.com

Additionally, we have a merch store! If you like any of the funny designs and want to purchase them as gifts on shirts, hoodies, mugs, phone cases, stickers, etc. just scan the QR code or click the link below:

https://www.redbubble.com/people/ChuckleChums/shop?asc=u

"Come and Laugh with Us!"

Other Books Sold on Our Amazon Store:

INTRO: WHY DAD JOKES ARE BOTH LOVED AND FEARED

Ah, the Dad Joke, the unsung hero of the comedic world. They can be as comforting as your favorite pair of old sneakers and simultaneously as uncomfortable as...well, your favorite pair of old sneakers. It's a conundrum, a mystery wrapped inside an enigma, served with a side of groans. But why, dear reader, do Dad Jokes elicit such a vast range of emotions? Let's buckle up and dive into this heartwarming and hilariously harrowing world.

The Loved: Warm Hugs in Verbal Form

1. **Memory Lane's Most Frequent Visitor**: Whenever a Dad Joke is unleashed, it's like revisiting the time when socks with sandals seemed like a good idea. They bring us back to those family gatherings, where Dad would stand up, clear his throat, and begin, "Did you hear about the math book? It has too many problems!"

2. **Universal Dad Code**: From the snowy peaks of Alaska to the sunny shores of Australia, Dad Jokes are the one constant. They're like the Wi-Fi of humor—connecting people from all corners of the globe.

3. **Safety First**: Dad Jokes are the seat belts of comedy. Sure, they might be a tad restrictive and occasionally dig into your side, but they're reliably safe. There's a sense of

security in knowing that a Dad Joke won't venture into the realm of the inappropriate.

The Feared: When Puns Strike Back

1. **Overdose Dangers**: Exposure to repeated Dad Jokes can lead to symptoms like uncontrollable eye-rolling, dramatic sighs, and the occasional "Dad, please stop." There's no known cure, and the condition may become chronic.

2. **Unexpected Ambush**: The dread of a public Dad Joke declaration is real. Be it at school events, friends' gatherings, or during that super-important meeting when your dad drops by unexpectedly and asks, "Why was the math book sad? Because it had too many problems!"

3. **Highly Contagious**: Once exposed, you may find yourself, against all logic, repeating these Dad Jokes. One minute you're laughing at Dad, the next you're whispering to your houseplants, "Hey, did you hear about the plant that went to school? It wanted to grow its knowledge!"

The Science(ish) Behind Dad Jokes

Research in a very non-existent laboratory has tried to decode the phenomenon of Dad Jokes. The findings? There's a direct correlation between the age of one's children and the frequency of Dad Jokes. Additionally, owning a lawnmower or a collection of ties with questionable patterns may also enhance the Dad Joke frequency.

Surviving in a Dad Joke Jungle

Navigating a world peppered with Dad Jokes requires skill, resilience, and a healthy dose of humor. Here's your survival guide:

1. **Master the Timely Exit**: Learn to recognize the signs. When Dad's eyes light up, and he begins with, "Did I

ever tell you about...", it might be your cue to suddenly remember an urgent task.

2. **Join the Dark Side**: Sometimes the best defense is a good offense. Arm yourself with a repertoire of Dad Jokes, and counter each of his with one of your own. "Dad, why don't eggs tell each other secrets? Because they might crack up!"

3. **Embrace the Inevitable**: At the end of the day, Dad Jokes, like mismatched socks or that weird jingle you can't get out of your head, are just part and parcel of life. Laugh, groan, and remember that these jokes come from a place of love... and an inexplicable love for puns.

In Defense of Dads (and Their Jokes)

Before we go any further, let's give our dads a break. Sure, their jokes might make us wish for a temporary loss of the hearing sense. But here's the thing: Dad Jokes come from a place of love. Each groan-worthy pun is a dad's attempt to connect, to bring a smile, or at least an exasperated sigh. They are tokens of love, wrapped in corny wit and delivered with unmatched enthusiasm.

Surviving (and Thriving) in a Dad Joke World

For those living in perpetual fear of the next Dad Joke ambush, here are some survival tips:

1. Develop an Early Warning System: Recognize the tell-tale signs: the glint in Dad's eyes, the sly grin, the clearing of the throat. When all signs align, brace yourself.

2. Counter with Your Own Dad Joke: Fight fire with fire! Retort with your own Dad Joke. "Dad, did you hear about the restaurant on the moon? Great food, no atmosphere!"

3. Acceptance is the Key: Understand that Dad Jokes, like taxes and embarrassing childhood photos, are inevitable. Embrace them, laugh (or groan) along, and

remember: one day, you might be the one delivering them!

Conclusion

Dad Jokes walk the tightrope between delight and despair. They're both the highlight of our day and the thing we jokingly (or not-so-jokingly) tease our dads about. But in a world full of uncertainties, there's one thing we can always count on: a dad somewhere, at this very moment, is making his child groan with a perfectly timed Dad Joke.

So the next time you hear, "How do you organize a space party? You planet!", give a nod of acknowledgment. Because behind every Dad Joke is a heart full of love, trying to sprinkle a little joy, one pun at a time.

CHAPTER 1: THE ORIGINS OF DAD JOKES—A BRIEF HISTORY AND PSYCHOLOGY

Before the dawn of civilization, before man figured out how to make fire or wheel, before language itself, there was something deeply ingrained in human culture. This primeval concept has sustained generations, defied critics, and made everyone from toddlers to teenagers roll their eyes. I'm talking, of course, about Dad Jokes.

Dad Jokes, those pun-tastic quips that only a father can tell without feeling immediate shame, have a history that stretches back further than you might think. Some historians speculate that the first Dad Joke ever told occurred when a caveman saw a rock and declared to his bewildered family, "This is my pet rock. He's a little boulder now!"

The phrase 'Dad Joke' might seem modern, but its roots go deep into the soil of human existence. Just like the ancient art of dad dancing and the time-honored tradition of dad snoring, Dad Jokes have evolved into an essential aspect of fatherhood.

The Dad Joke in Ancient Civilizations

Let's take a time-traveling adventure through history and explore how Dad Jokes have shaped civilizations and empires.

Ancient Egypt

In the sands of ancient Egypt, where the pharaohs ruled and the Nile flowed like the tears of children hearing a Dad Joke, there's evidence that even they weren't spared from the punny onslaught. Hieroglyphics have been translated to reveal that one pharaoh inscribed, "Why did the mummy call for a timeout? Because he felt he was coming unraveled!" The scholars deciphering these inscriptions were so dismayed that they almost called a 'dad' cease-fire.

Classical Greece

Ah, the Greeks—philosophers, poets, and pioneers of drama. What many don't know is that Socrates was an aficionado of the Dad Joke. While the official records never made it to the mainstream, we have it on good authority that he was overheard telling a young Plato, "Why do we never tell secrets on a farm? Because the potatoes have eyes, the corn has ears, and the beans stalk."

Plato did not include this in his dialogues, possibly due to the potential damage it would cause to his mentor's reputation. The only thing worse than drinking poison, it seems, is hearing a Dad Joke you can never unhear.

The Middle Ages

During medieval times, knights and serfs alike were subjected to the oral tradition of Dad Jokes. When King Arthur pulled Excalibur from the stone, a dad knight at the Round Table supposedly quipped, "Looks like Arthur is a real cut-up!" The joke was so poorly received that the knight was promptly assigned latrine duty.

The Science of the Dad Joke

Why, oh why, do dads insist on telling these jokes? This phenomenon has puzzled psychologists, anthropologists, and weary family members for years. Some theories suggest that Dad Jokes are a form of bonding. You see, laughter—or in this case, forced laughter—is a universal human experience.

The Dad Joke Reflex

Scientists have discovered a psychological underpinning that might explain the persistence of Dad Jokes: the Dad Joke Reflex. According to experts, this is an uncontrollable urge in dads to make puns, no matter how inappropriate the timing or cringe-inducing the content. Some suggest that the Dad Joke Reflex developed as a survival mechanism, a way for early human fathers to attract the attention of their children and teach them crucial skills, like how to be really, really, annoying.

The 'Eye-Roll' Response

Now, you might wonder, why do we often respond to Dad Jokes with an eye-roll? Is it a biological countermeasure? Indeed, it is. The Eye-Roll Response is a defense mechanism that we adapted to protect the human brain from cringing too hard. When a dad begins a joke with, "Why did the chicken cross the road?", the eye-roll is your brain's way of saying, "I've seen this one coming, and I'm taking protective measures."

The Modern Era

In the present day, the Dad Joke has found new mediums to infect—I mean, to delight—the masses. Social media, texting, and unfortunately, even PowerPoint presentations at work have become the fertile ground for Dad Jokes to sprout like weeds you never wanted in your garden.

The Rise of the 'Dad Joke Meme'

We can't talk about modernity without acknowledging the viral nature of the Dad Joke Meme. These are cleverly crafted jokes that travel from screen to screen, making millions of people simultaneously groan. Thanks to the internet, a dad joke can be delivered, suffered, and forwarded thousands of times in a matter of minutes. It's like a pandemic, but you can't even wear a mask to protect yourself.

The Dad Joke Olympics

Yes, you read it right. There's even an international competition now where dads from all over the world compete for the title of

"The World's Best Dad Joke Teller." The winner receives a golden spatula and a lifetime supply of socks and sandals. Categories include "Best One-Liner," "Most Groan-Inducing Pun," and "Best Joke Told at an Inappropriate Time," like during a wedding toast or a solemn gathering.

Conclusion

The Dad Joke has become a cornerstone of humor, spanning across cultures, languages, and eras. From the hieroglyphics of ancient Egypt to the Twitter feeds of today, Dad Jokes are here to stay. They're the jokes that make you groan but also the ones that you secretly love, or at least, can't escape.

So the next time your dad, uncle, or any paternal figure begins a sentence with, "I've got a joke for you," remember, you're not just hearing a silly pun. You're experiencing a rich, cultural artifact that has withstood the test of time. The Dad Joke is an eternal flame—burning, irritating, but ultimately warming the very cockles of our hearts.

CHAPTER 2: THE ANATOMY OF A DAD JOKE

The Dad Joke, a riddle wrapped in a mystery inside an enigma, seasoned generously with puns, and served in the platter of family gatherings. If jokes were people, the Dad Joke would be that weird uncle who shows up uninvited to family events, eats all the snacks, and then proceeds to perform magic tricks with napkins. You can't decide whether to kick him out or give him a standing ovation.

But what is it that makes a Dad Joke a Dad Joke? Is it the puns, the groans they induce, or the unmistakable dad chuckle that follows? Is it an art, a science, or a misdemeanor? Are Dad Jokes just failed regular jokes, or are they a highly specialized form of humor that has adapted and survived over millennia?

My friends, we are about to dive into an investigation so profound that it may forever change how you view that person you call "Dad," "Papa," or "Hey You, Fix This." We're talking deep, deep, psychological stuff here—think Freud but with more punchlines and fewer cigars.

The Recipe: Ingredients of a Dad Joke

The Buildup: Or, the Coiled Spring

The "set-up" of a Dad Joke is the equivalent of the wind-up of a jack-in-the-box; it's the coiled spring, the calm before the storm, the appetizer that precedes the regrettable entree. It usually comes in the form of a seemingly innocent question or a misleadingly straightforward statement. Examples include, "Why did the chicken cross the road?" or "I used to play piano by ear..."

The Pause: Suspense in the Air

Between the setup and the punchline lies a sacred realm known as "the pause." This pause is the vacuum in which all the cosmic energies of the Dad Joke universe coalesce. It's like the zero in mathematics: seemingly empty, but holding infinite possibilities. The pause is what separates the amateurs from the dad-joke virtuosos. Nail the pause, and you've got your audience trapped like fish in a very corny net.

The Punchline: Cue Eye Rolls

Ah, the punchline. The punchline is to a Dad Joke what a plot twist is to a soap opera: utterly predictable yet disarmingly shocking. The punchline usually involves a pun, a play on words, or an observation so glaringly obvious that it somehow becomes profound.

For example, after the setup of "I used to play piano by ear," comes the punchline, "but now I use my hands." If you heard a soft thud, don't be alarmed; that was just the sound of a joke landing flat on its face, only to get up and say, "Tada!"

The Laugh: Trademark of Dadhood

Every Dad Joke is followed by a dad chuckle, which is like a regular laugh but with more self-satisfaction and less social awareness. This laugh is usually loud enough for the whole family to hear but subtle enough not to awaken the ancient spirits that were put to rest by ancestors who never had to endure such jokes.

The Life Cycle of a Dad Joke

Much like the butterfly, a Dad Joke goes through several stages of development:

Birth: The "Eureka" Moment

Every Dad Joke begins as a tiny idea in a dad's mind, like a pearl inside an oyster or a burp inside a soda can. This usually happens during crucial moments like fixing a leaky faucet, attending a PTA meeting, or pretending to listen to your day.

Adolescence: The Trial Phase

Before a Dad Joke can be unleashed upon the world, it must first be tested. This usually occurs in safe, controlled environments, such as the dinner table or the car (because where can you run?). If it survives this stage, the Dad Joke is ready for the world. If not, it goes back into the lab for further "development," much like the rejected prototypes of superhero gadgets.

Adulthood: The Social Media Phase

In today's tech-savvy world, a successful Dad Joke often finds its way to social media, where it either goes viral or gets buried under cat videos. Either way, its destiny is fulfilled.

Old Age: The Revival

Like fashion trends and retro music, old Dad Jokes never die; they merely fade away, waiting for the right time to make a comeback. What was groan-worthy in the '90s could be ironically hilarious in the 2020s. Or not. But that's a risk a dad is willing to take.

The Impact: A Sociological Exploration

In a society increasingly dependent on digital communication, the Dad Joke serves as a reminder of our roots. It's a callback to the days when humor was simple, conversations were real, and text messages were things you scribbled in secret codes during class.

In many ways, Dad Jokes serve as cultural equalizers. They transcend geography, age, and taste, appealing—or appalling—to a vast range of people, from kids who giggle at anything to adults who have seen enough of life to find absurdity in simplicity.

Conclusion: The Enigma Continues

To understand the anatomy of a Dad Joke is to peek into the very soul of human society. It reflects our shared history, our collective consciousness, and our universal need to roll our eyes at something. But most importantly, the Dad Joke is a testament to the spirit of fatherhood—a unique blend of wisdom, playfulness, and an undying love for puns. And though we may groan, sigh, or even retaliate with jokes of our own, one thing is certain: the Dad Joke is here to stay, in all its groan-inducing glory.

So, the next time you hear the familiar words, "Hey, want to hear a joke?" take a deep breath, muster a smile, and brace yourself for the inevitable. Because whether you like it or not, the Dad Joke is an unchangeable part of the human experience, as constant as the stars, as enduring as dad sneakers, and as everlasting as that stain on the living room carpet that nobody wants to talk about.

And remember, dissecting a Dad Joke is like dissecting a frog; you may understand it better, but the frog dies in the process. Similarly, overanalyzing a Dad Joke may rob it of its simplistic charm. Then again, does it really have any charm to lose? Ah, the enigma continues.

That's it, folks! You've just survived the most extensive, exhaustive, and possibly exhausting exploration of the Dad Joke. If you've made it this far without rolling your eyes into another dimension or questioning your life choices, give yourself a pat on the back. You're either incredibly brave, or you might just be a dad in the making. Either way, may the puns be with you!

CHAPTER 3: THE IMPACT ON FAMILY DYNAMICS

Welcome back, brave souls, as we continue our expedition through the uproarious wilderness known as the Land of Dad Jokes. With your muskets of wisdom and shields of eye-rolls, we now march toward a yet-unexplored territory—the intricate ecosystem of Family Dynamics. Imagine a garden, but instead of flowers and herbs, you've got groans, chuckles, and life lessons seasoned with puns.

The Royal Court of Family Life

In a well-functioning monarchy of comedy, Dad Jokes serve as the court jesters. They occupy a unique place, sometimes the center of attention and sometimes banished to the outskirts. But like any self-respecting jester, a Dad Joke knows how to make a comeback, usually during Sunday brunch or a long car drive.

The Queen Mother: The First Audience

The Queen Mother, or simply 'Mom,' is often the first test audience for a budding Dad Joke. She is the Simon Cowell of this talent show—the judge who's seen it all and is rarely impressed, yet occasionally breaks into a smile that says, "Alright, that was corny, but cute."

The Princess and the Pea (and the Pun)

Ah, the children. They are the unsuspecting victims and

beneficiaries of the Dad Joke Kingdom. Their reactions range from adoring giggles to rebellious eye-rolls, often within the same minute. The impact of Dad Jokes on kids is as varied as their favorite cereal choices, and almost as controversial.

The Pet: The Silent Bearer

Don't underestimate the four-legged or finned family members. Whether it's a dog, cat, or a low-maintenance goldfish, pets are often the silent audience to the stand-up routine that is Dad's life. Their thoughts on Dad Jokes remain a mystery, but it's safe to assume they are contemplating the meaning of existence—or at least the schedule for their next meal.

Social Gatherings: Where Dad Jokes Roam Free

Nothing says 'family event' like the unleashing of a Dad Joke arsenal. Be it birthdays, anniversaries, or the 'just-because-I-can' BBQs, Dad Jokes are like the embarrassing dance moves—awaiting their grand reveal.

The BBQ Quagmire

Ah, the family BBQ, the place where Dad Jokes multiply like a species trying to avoid extinction. "Why did the tofu cross the road? To prove it wasn't chicken!" Hilarious, right? No? Well, that won't stop Dad from trying again when he's flipping burgers.

The Holiday Hullabaloo

Holidays are to Dad Jokes what sunlight is to Superman—an almost magical source of power. "What did one Christmas ornament say to the other? 'You crack me up!'" Cue the collective facepalms, disguised as holiday face rubs to alleviate stress.

The Joke Economy: Supply, Demand, and Inflation

Let's not forget the economic aspect of Dad Jokes within the family unit. Yes, you heard me right. There is an underground economy of Dad Jokes, and you're all part of it.

Supply and Demand

Dads supply the jokes, and whether you like it or not, you demand them—subconsciously, perhaps, but demand them you do. It's a never-ending loop of awkward chuckles and sighs of resignation.

The Joke Inflation

Ever heard the same Dad Joke more than once? Of course, you have. Like any economy facing an oversupply, the value of a repeatedly used Dad Joke undergoes severe depreciation. A joke that once elicited hearty laughs soon gets eye-rolls, contributing to what economists in imaginary universities call "Joke Inflation."

The Unexpected Lessons: Wisdom in Disguise

Unbelievable as it may seem, Dad Jokes often carry shards of wisdom, like nuggets of gold in a turbulent river of words.

Survival in the Dad Joke Wilderness: A Guide

Living in a family inundated with Dad Jokes is a bit like surviving in the wilderness—you need skills, patience, and an excellent sense of humor.

1. **The Art of Deflection**: Learn to deflect a Dad Joke with another joke, sarcasm, or a subject change. "Dad, what's for dinner?" "Leftovers." "Ah, the meal that keeps on giving!"

2. **The Counter-Joke Attack**: Fight fire with fire. Respond to a Dad Joke with a joke of your own. You might not win, but you'll earn respect and possibly reduce the frequency of incoming jokes.

3. **The Fake Laugh**: Sometimes, it's just easier to pretend. A fake laugh can be your white flag when you're too tired to engage. Warning: May encourage more jokes.

In Conclusion: The Butterfly Effect

The impact of Dad Jokes on family dynamics is a multi-layered tapestry, sewn with threads of laughter, groans, and life lessons. It's a shared history, a bonding ritual, and a rite of passage, all rolled into one.

In the grand scheme of things, a Dad Joke might seem as

inconsequential as a butterfly flapping its wings. But as chaos theory suggests, even the smallest flap can cause a tornado on the other side of the world—or at least a whirlwind of reactions at the family dinner table.

So let's raise a toast to Dad Jokes—the condiment that adds flavor to the staple diet of family life. They may not be to everyone's taste, but hey, neither is fruitcake, and we've been gifting that for centuries.

As we close this chapter on a topic as rich and complex as a double-layered dad-bod, remember this: A family that groans together, stays together. Or at least has something to talk—or laugh—about. Cheers to that!

CHAPTER 4: CASE STUDIES: THE GOOD, THE BAD, AND THE UGLY

Ah, the case study: the staple of scholarly work, the bread and butter of academia, and the holy grail of proving points that no one really questioned in the first place. But when it comes to Dad Jokes, you see, case studies are like fine wine paired with fast food—somewhat unexpected, but utterly delightful.

So put on your lab coats, your thinking caps, or your comfiest sweatpants, and join us in this scientific(ish) investigation as we dissect real-life instances of Dad Jokes in their natural habitats. In other words, prepare yourself for the laughs, the cringes, and the "Oh, why did he say that?!"

Case Study 1: The Good – The Dad at the Grocery Store

The Background:

Meet Steve, a father of two, taking his kids on the proverbial "weekly hunting and gathering" expedition to the local grocery store. Steve is armed with a shopping list in one hand and a carton of dad jokes in the other, ready for action.

The Execution:

Steve maneuvers the cart down the cereal aisle and spots the breakfast grains. "Why did the cereal break up with milk?" he quips, eyes twinkling. Before his kids can answer, Steve delivers the punchline: "Because it felt like it was drowning in a toxic relationship!"

The Aftermath:

To his surprise, his children, Sarah and Timmy, burst out laughing. Sarah later recounts this joke to her friends at school, earning her a temporary reputation as the 'cool joke girl.' Steve basks in the glory of his Dad Joke success.

Analysis:

A textbook example of a good Dad Joke. Timely, thematic, and relatable, the joke transcends generational boundaries and strengthens family ties.

Case Study 2: The Bad – The Family Game Night Debacle

The Background:

It's Friday night, and the Johnson family has assembled for a high-stakes game of Monopoly. Dad, alias Bill, sees this as an opportunity for unleashing his brand-new Dad Jokes, each one tailored for the occasion.

Execution:

As his daughter lands on the infamous Boardwalk property laden with hotels, Bill sees his golden opportunity. "Why did the Monopoly man go to therapy?" he asks. Sensing doom, his family hesitates, but Bill proceeds, "Because he realized his life was always up for auction, and he was never in 'control'!"

The Aftermath:

His daughter immediately declares bankruptcy and leaves the room. His son contemplates swapping the Monopoly money for real cash and fleeing the country. Bill's wife contemplates whether it's too late to switch to a game of Scrabble, where words, at least, have point values that can be quantified.

Analysis:

The Dad Joke was too intricate for the casual setting and touched upon existential ideas that were too deep for a family trying to swindle each other out of fake money. A clear miss.

Case Study 3: The Ugly – The School Talent Show

The Background:

The school gym is packed with parents, kids, and an unbearable amount of stage smoke from the previous magic act gone wrong. Dennis, father of young Emma, is emceeing the event and feels that the show lacks some Dad Joke flair.

The Execution:

Dennis steps up to the mic. "Why did the music teacher go to jail?" he projects, smiling like a Cheshire cat. The crowd is dead silent, either in anticipation or dread. "Because she got caught with too many sharp objects!" Dennis booms.

The Aftermath:

The joke lands with a thud heavier than a dropped tuba. Emma considers joining the Foreign Legion just to escape the embarrassment. The music teacher in attendance debates between filing a formal complaint and challenging Dennis to a duel with musical instruments.

Analysis:

High-risk environment, questionable joke topic, and poor timing. The Dad Joke was not only unfunny but also teetered on the edge of inappropriateness. An epic fail, this one goes down in the annals of Dad Joke history as "The Ugly."

A Comparative Analysis: What We've Learned

1. **Environment Matters**: Choose your battleground wisely. A grocery store may be a more forgiving stage than a school talent show.

2. **Know Your Audience**: What might make your kids laugh could potentially traumatize them in another setting. Adapt to the mood and the crowd.

3. **Timing is Everything**: Like a predator sensing the right

moment to pounce on its prey, a dad must sense the right moment to unleash a Dad Joke.

4. **Simplicity is Key**: Don't overcomplicate a Dad Joke. The charm often lies in its simplicity, much like a stick figure drawing or a potato.

Conclusion: A Kaleidoscope of Reactions

Dad Jokes are to family dynamics what spices are to cooking— a little can go a long way, but the wrong one can ruin the dish. They can bring laughter, foster bonds, and sometimes make you question your family ties, all within the span of a few seconds.

Whether they're hits or misses, Dad Jokes are like those embarrassing childhood photos your parents keep in the living room—they may not always make you look good, but they're an indelible part of your history.

And so, we close this compendium of Dad Joke case studies, each more enlightening (or bewildering) than the last. As you ponder the profound impact of Dad Jokes on human civilization, consider this—maybe the real Dad Joke was the friends and awkward family moments we made along the way.

As always, may your life be filled with laughter, groans, and a hearty dose of "Oh Dad, why?!"

CHAPTER 5: THE SCIENCE OF THE GROAN

The groan—the universal language of Dad Joke sufferers, the call of the wild teenager, and the lament of the spouses who know they're in for a lifetime of puns. This vocal phenomenon is as mysterious as the Bermuda Triangle and as enigmatic as the reasoning behind wearing socks with sandals. In this chapter, we shall attempt to decode the science behind the groan, or as it's known in academic circles, the "Audible Sigh of Despair."

The Anatomy of a Groan: It's All About the Vibrations

Like a well-crafted cocktail, the groan has various layers:

1. **The Inception**: It all starts with the brain recognizing the incoming Dad Joke, much like a meteorologist detects an approaching storm. Alarm bells go off, signaling the vocal cords to prepare for action.

2. **The Build-Up**: As the joke's punchline approaches, tension rises. The lungs fill up with air, awaiting the brain's signal. It's the calm before the groan.

3. **The Release**: Finally, as the punchline hits, the groan escapes the lips in a beautiful cacophony of resignation and despair. A well-executed groan may last anywhere from 0.5 to 3 seconds, depending on the joke's perceived threat level.

4. **The Resonance**: A highly impactful groan might inspire solidarity groans, creating a chorus of social harmony. It's almost poetic, really.

The Types of Groans: A Field Guide

Not all groans are created equal. Understanding the nuanced differences can help you better navigate the social labyrinth of Dad Jokes.

1. **The Polite Groan**: A low, soft noise, emitted to acknowledge the Dad Joke without encouraging more. It's the "Thanks, but no thanks" of groans.

2. **The Resigned Groan**: This one is usually longer, indicating a sort of surrender to the inevitability of Dad Jokes in one's life. It's the white flag in the endless battle of wits.

3. **The Exaggerated Groan**: This groan is a theatrical performance, loud and long enough to disrupt local air traffic. This is less about the Dad Joke and more about sending a message: "Stop, for the love of sanity!"

4. **The Silent Groan**: No audible sound, just a long exhale, sometimes accompanied by an eye roll. It's the ninja of groans—stealthy, but deadly.

The Doppler Effect: How Groans Travel

In physics, the Doppler effect explains why a car engine sounds differently as it approaches and then passes you. Similarly, the Dad Joke Groan seems to change in pitch and intensity as it moves through a room. The groan usually starts low, gathers volume as it reaches peak embarrassment, and then fades away, leaving behind an awkward silence and a dad who's probably plotting his next joke.

The Impact on Family Dynamics: The Domino Effect

The groan is more than just a sound; it's an event, a spectacle that can dramatically shift the power dynamics in a family setting.

A well-timed groan can halt a Dad Joke spree, while a poorly executed one might embolden the dad to unleash a whole arsenal of new jokes, often saved for moments when the groan shields are down.

The Groan as a Defense Mechanism: To Groan or Not to Groan?

Is groaning an effective strategy to counter Dad Jokes? Studies (conducted by imaginary scientists in theoretical labs) show mixed results:

1. **Pros**: Groaning provides an immediate emotional release, like popping the bubble wrap of the soul.
2. **Cons**: Groaning might be misinterpreted as a signal to continue, a laugh in disguise, encouraging an unending cycle of Dad Jokes.

The Groan in Popular Culture: Breaking the Sound Barrier

The groan has made its way into books, movies, and even memes. It's a universal symbol of mild suffering, akin to the cry of a wolf baying at the moon or a poet writing verses about unrequited love. In both cases, the message is clear: "Why are you doing this to me?"

Conclusion: The Beautiful Complexity of the Simple Groan

The groan is both an art form and a science, a complex psychological response boiled down to a simple vocalization. It's the symphony of resignation, the sonnet of surrender, and the haiku of despair—all wrapped in one.

It might seem like a trivial part of our daily lives, but don't underestimate the power of a well-timed groan. It's the closest thing we have to a universal language, uniting us all in the shared experience of hearing a Dad Joke and living to groan about it.

So the next time you find yourself at the receiving end of a Dad Joke, remember that your groan contributes to a rich tapestry of social interactions and familial bonds. It's a small but significant rebellion, a flag of individuality planted on the moon of domestic life. Groan loud, groan proud, and may your vocal cords stay strong in the face of incoming Dad Jokes.

And there you have it, dear readers. You've now earned a theoretical Ph.D. in Groanology. Wear it as a badge of honor, for life is filled with Dad Jokes, and the groan is your trusty shield. Now go out there and groan like nobody's listening, because, let's be honest, they're probably not—they're too busy groaning themselves.

CHAPTER 6: THE ART OF DELIVERY

Ladies, gentlemen, and connoisseurs of corny humor, brace yourselves. We're diving headfirst into the heart of the Dad Joke universe: the art of delivery. This is where the rubber meets the road, the yolk meets the eggshell, and the dad meets...the moment of truth.

You see, a Dad Joke is like a soufflé. It may have the right ingredients, but if the oven's temperature fluctuates too much, you're left with something resembling scrambled eggs with delusions of grandeur. Similarly, the success or catastrophic failure of a Dad Joke hinges on its delivery. So, let's dissect this intriguing art form with the seriousness it...um, doesn't really deserve, but let's pretend it does.

The Stage is Set: A Dad's Natural Habitat

Before we talk about delivery, we must consider the setting. It's a sunny afternoon, perhaps, and Dad is tending to his pride and joy—no, not you, the lawn! The neighbor waves hello, setting the stage for a Dad Joke. "Why did the lawn feel self-conscious?" Dad asks, a smile creeping onto his face. "Because it was always getting mowed down!"

The birds stop chirping, the Earth's rotation slows, and for a brief moment, the universe contemplates reversing the Big Bang. Yes, the setting plays a vital role.

Vocal Inflection: The Highs and Lows

The tone is crucial. A flat delivery can kill a joke faster than a teenager's attention span during a lecture on table manners. If the tone rises towards the end, the audience is psychologically prompted to respond—typically, in the form of a laugh, a groan, or an existential crisis.

Timing: The Pause, the Rush, and the Eternal Wait

Ah, timing! In the world of Dad Jokes, timing is like the cherry on top of a questionable dessert—you didn't ask for it, but it sure makes things more interesting.

1. **The Pause**: As discussed in the anatomy of a Dad Joke, the pause is where potential energy builds, akin to a roller coaster climbing to its apex.

2. **The Rush**: This is when the punchline is delivered rapidly, barely giving you time to brace for impact. It's the comedic equivalent of ripping off a band-aid.

3. **The Eternal Wait**: Here, the joke meanders, taking its sweet time, like a snail contemplating the meaning of life. Just when you think the punchline will never come, it hits, and the room is filled with the echoes of anticlimactic relief.

Body Language: The Physical Comedy of a Dad Joke

Much like interpretive dance or mime, a Dad Joke often includes physical elements.

1. **The Hand Gestures**: A pointed finger, a slap of the knee, or an elaborate swirl of the arm can add flavor. Just ensure you're not within slapping distance of fragile objects.

2. **Facial Expressions**: The eye twinkle, the eyebrow wiggle, and the mouth's gradual transformation into a grin are all part of the Dad Joke ecosystem.

3. **The Exit**: Sometimes, a quick exit can salvage even the most catastrophic Dad Joke. Picture this: Dad delivers

the joke, waits a beat, then slowly moonwalks out of the room, leaving the family in a state of bewildered amusement.

Props: Because Sometimes Words Just Aren't Enough

A Dad Joke can sometimes include props: a whoopee cushion, a fake spider, or even a strategically placed piece of fruit. "Orange you glad I didn't say banana?" Dad chortles, revealing the actual orange he's been hiding behind his back.

Advanced Techniques: The Callback and the Series

Seasoned Dad Joke artists sometimes employ advanced techniques.

1. **The Callback**: This is when a Dad Joke refers back to a previous joke or incident, creating a sort of inside joke that outsiders will never understand and insiders wish they didn't.

2. **The Series**: Here, one Dad Joke leads to another, forming a series or saga. It's like a TV show that keeps getting renewed for seasons no one asked for.

The Side Effects: Immediate and Long-Term

While immediate reactions to a Dad Joke might include laughter, groans, or a sudden desire to join a witness protection program, the long-term effects are more complex:

1. **Bonding**: Believe it or not, Dad Jokes can create memorable family moments. These are the stories you'll retell, either as cherished memories or cautionary tales for future generations.

2. **Skill Transfer**: Children and spouses exposed to frequent Dad Jokes often become adept at delivering them too. It's like learning to make lemonade out of the lemons life—or Dad—throws at you.

3. **Life Lessons**: Sometimes, believe it or not, Dad Jokes carry a nugget of wisdom wrapped in a blanket of

absurdity. "Why don't scientists trust atoms?" Dad asks. "Because they make up everything!" Somewhere in that cringeworthy punchline lies a lesson about trust and skepticism.

The Critics: A Word on Reception

Ah, critics—they're the ones who decide whether a Dad Joke will be enshrined in the Hall of Fame or buried in the Tomb of the Unknown Joke. Critics come in various forms: the supportive mom, the eye-rolling teenager, the laughing toddler, and the indifferent pet. Each has their criteria, ranging from "At least you tried" to "Please move out."

Conclusion: The Mona Lisa of Jokes

Delivering a Dad Joke is like painting a miniature Mona Lisa on a grain of rice using only a toothpick and three dollops of paint. It's an art form that requires precision, courage, and a healthy dose of delusion. And much like art, its beauty—or horror—is in the eye of the beholder.

So the next time you're on the receiving end of a Dad Joke, take a moment to appreciate the intricate ballet that just unfolded before you. The stage, the delivery, the timing, the props, and the impact —all of it culminates in a performance that lasts but a few seconds but lingers in memory like the aroma of a strong cheese: not always pleasant, but certainly unforgettable.

And there you have it, an in-depth look at the complex, bewildering, and undeniably fascinating art of delivering a Dad Joke. If you've made it this far, congratulations! You're now qualified to judge the Annual International Dad Joke Championships, an event that absolutely should exist, even if it doesn't.

As always, may your days be filled with laughter, your nights with restful sleep, and your life with a manageable amount of Dad Jokes. Take care, and keep on groaning!

CHAPTER 7: DAD JOKES IN THE DIGITAL AGE

Ah, the digital age—where information travels at the speed of light, and Dad Jokes travel even faster, thanks to social media platforms, group chats, and those chain emails your uncle insists on sending every Tuesday. Today, we shall explore this brave new world where technology has unlocked unprecedented levels of eye-rolling and facepalming. This is like the Silicon Valley of Dad Jokes, minus the lucrative IPOs.

The Rise of the Meme: A Picture is Worth a Thousand Groans

Once upon a time, Dad Jokes were confined to family gatherings, long road trips, or any place where the audience was a captive one—sometimes literally. But memes have freed Dad Jokes from these physical constraints, enabling them to spread like digital wildfire or a virtual virus, depending on your perspective.

Imagine a photo of a potato with the caption, "I yam what I yam!" That's it. That's the meme. And before you know it, it has thousands of likes, shares, and an invitation to be a guest speaker at a vegetable rights rally. Welcome to 2023.

Hashtags: The Calling Cards of Modern-Day Dad Jokes

Hashtags are like the spices of social media cuisine. A well-chosen hashtag can give a Dad Joke that extra zing, while a poorly chosen one can make it go down like a lead balloon—or a dad trying to breakdance.

For example, a Dad Joke about coffee could be accompanied by hashtags like #JavaDadJokes, #EspressoYourself, or #GrindPuns. Within seconds, the joke becomes part of multiple online communities, much like a culinary dish being entered into various categories at a food fair. Mind you, it may not win any prizes, but it's participating that counts, right?

Viral Videos: When Dad Jokes Become Box Office Hits

YouTube has given dads a platform to broadcast their humor like never before. Forget the grainy camcorder footage of your school plays; now dads can create full-blown productions to deliver their jokes. Picture this: a dad dressed as a barista, serving coffee in a homemade set resembling a café, just to set up his one-liner: "Why did the coffee file a complaint? It was getting mugged every day!"

Will it go viral? Probably not. But will it get at least five views from various family members? Absolutely. And for many dads, that's just as good as an Oscar.

Podcasts: The Unsung Heroes of the Dad Joke World

Move over, true crime and political commentary; the Dad Joke Podcasts have arrived. These audio gems are the perfect medium for the dad who loves the sound of his voice almost as much as his jokes. Episodes often feature segments like "Pun of the Week," "Groaner Alerts," and "Listeners' Choice," where fans can submit their Dad Jokes, creating a sense of community and shared suffering.

Dad Joke Bots: The Future is Now, and It's Hilarious

The advancements in AI have led to the inevitable: Dad Joke Bots. Yes, now you can get your daily dose of dad humor without the accompanying lecture on how to change a tire. Simply type "Tell me a joke" and behold as the bot responds with something like, "Why did the computer go to therapy? It had too many issues!"

It's worth noting that the Dad Joke Bot does not (yet) possess the ability to laugh at its own jokes. Perhaps that's the final frontier for AI—to understand not just the structure of humor, but also the nuanced art of the self-satisfied chuckle.

The Ethical Dilemmas: To Share or Not to Share

In the digital age, a Dad Joke can be screenshot, shared, and sent around the world in less time than it takes to say, "Pull my finger." But with great power comes great responsibility. Unauthorized sharing of Dad Jokes can lead to fame or infamy, often depending on the audience's collective mood.

In a worst-case scenario, a bad Dad Joke could get "ratioed," receiving more negative comments than likes or retweets. Imagine posting a joke like, "Why did the scarecrow get promoted? He was outstanding in his field!" only to find it inundated with comments like, "Dad, stop. Just stop." A word of caution: think before you share—or at least be prepared for the merciless judgment of the Internet.

Influencer Dads: When Dad Jokes Become Brand Deals

Believe it or not, some dads have leveraged their penchant for Dad Jokes into lucrative brand deals. Picture an Instagram post where a dad stands next to a lawnmower, holding a sign that reads, "This machine is a real 'cut-up'! #Ad #MowDadJokes #GrassIsAlwaysPunnier." Yes, it's a thing. Welcome to the future, where even puns can be monetized.

Conclusion: The Digital Footprint of a Timeless Art Form

Dad Jokes have proven remarkably adaptable, evolving with the times while retaining their classic, corny essence. The digital age has given these jokes a platform to reach a global audience, for better or worse.

In a world teeming with conflict, challenges, and never-ending updates to our phone's operating system, perhaps we need Dad Jokes more than ever. They remind us of simpler times, offering a nostalgic respite, like a digital comfort food for the soul—equally loved and feared, shared and regretted, eye-rolled at and chuckled with.

So, the next time you come across a Dad Joke meme, pause for a moment before hitting that share button. Know that you're part of a grand tradition, a worldwide network of groaners and chucklers, united by the irresistible allure of a bad joke told with good intentions. In that sense, we're all dad-jokesters in the making, contributing to a legacy as enduring as the jokes are ephemeral.

And there you have it! You've survived yet another chapter in this deep dive into the world of Dad Jokes. If you've made it this far, congratulations! You're now a certified expert in the field of digital Dad Jokery, an honor only surpassed by getting a verified checkmark on Twitter.

May your timelines be ever filled with chuckles, your memes be forever dank, and your puns always find a willing audience, online and off. Until next time, keep those hashtags ready and those GIFs loaded. The digital frontier of Dad Jokes awaits!

CHAPTER 8: THE ETHICS OF DAD JOKING

Welcome, esteemed scholars of silliness, philosophers of the pun, and ethicists of the eye-roll. If you've made it to Chapter 8, you are either seriously committed to understanding Dad Jokes, or you're doing everything you can to avoid actual work. Either way, I salute you. This chapter aims to explore the ethics surrounding Dad Jokes. Yes, you read that correctly. Sit down, fasten your seatbelt, and prepare for a journey into the moral maze of this unique form of humor.

Is It Ever "Too Soon"?: Timing the Untimely

The primary ethical conundrum surrounding Dad Jokes is timing. We've all heard the phrase "too soon," which can also be applied to Dad Jokes. Let's consider a hypothetical:

Your neighbor's pet parrot escapes. During the extensive neighborhood search for the bird, your neighbor rings your doorbell. You answer, and before any semblance of sensitivity can kick in, you blurt out, "I guess Polly doesn't want a cracker, huh?"

Was it too soon? Likely. Does the joke land you in 'Neighborly Purgatory'? Absolutely.

The Location Quandary: Not All Places are Joking Places

When it comes to location, Dad Jokes operate on a peculiar ethical plane. A Dad Joke during a family dinner might be welcomed or at least tolerated. However, busting out a pun at a solemn event? You might find yourself on the fast track to Social Pariahville.

Just imagine unveiling this gem at a job interview: "Why did the spreadsheet go to therapy? Because it had too many 'cells'!" Cue awkward silence and a swift escort to the door by security.

Puns and Political Correctness: A Tightrope Walk

The realm of Dad Jokes is not immune to the broader discussions surrounding political correctness. Here, we face another ethical fork in the road. Is a joke that's purely intended for laughs, yet skirts the line of political correctness, acceptable or not?

Consider the Dad Joke about the muffin at a weight loss seminar: "Why did the muffin do a workout? To turn into a 'buff'in!" It's cheesy, innocuous, and yet could be considered insensitive in certain contexts. A Dad Joke told in bad taste can turn from a light chuckle to a heavy groan quite quickly.

The Environmental Impact: The Carbon Footprint of a Dad Joke

Believe it or not, Dad Jokes have an environmental impact. Each groan, eye-roll, or gasp of disbelief emits carbon dioxide into the atmosphere. If we add up the global total of Dad Jokes told daily (an estimated 983,423,764 jokes per day, according to a study conducted by the University of Totally Made-Up Statistics), we can only conclude that Dad Jokes contribute to global warming. This, dear friends, is the inconvenient truth Al Gore forgot to mention.

The Unwanted Sequel: When Does a Dad Joke Become Harassment?

Like a summer blockbuster nobody asked for, Dad Jokes can sometimes overstay their welcome. When does a Dad Joke cross the line from innocent banter into the realm of harassment? Consider the office setting, a battleground of conflicting humor norms. You may find your Dad Joke about the copier being "out of paper and out of hope" to be a knee-slapper. However, the HR department might see it as an HR nightmare.

Age-Appropriateness: When Do You Expose the Youth?

Many a parent has grappled with the ethical dilemma of when to introduce Dad Jokes to their offspring. Do you wait until they're mature enough to grasp the subtleties of irony? Or do you begin immediately, building their tolerance from an early age, like a vaccine against bad humor? It's a tough call and one that could shape a child's sense of humor for years to come.

The Self-Inflicted Dad Joke: A New Ethical Frontier

It's not only others who can be the target of Dad Jokes; sometimes, Dads themselves are the punchline. When a dad intentionally employs self-deprecating humor, does it cancel out the ethical concerns surrounding timing, location, and appropriateness? After all, if the joker is also the jokee, it's sort of like an ethical 'buy one, get one free,' isn't it?

The Consent Factor: Should Warnings be Issued?

Should people be warned before being subjected to a Dad Joke? Could something akin to the "Explicit Content" sticker for music albums be applicable here? Picture a "Contains Dad Jokes" warning label affixed to a dad before entering a social event. It might not prevent the telling of the joke, but at least it would allow for informed groaning.

Conclusion: An Ethical Quagmire or a Moral Molehill?

As we have traversed the murky waters of Dad Joke ethics, it's become clear that the subject is fraught with moral pitfalls and ethical quagmires. Yet, isn't that what makes Dad Jokes so universally human? They embody the

CHAPTER 9: EMBRACING YOUR INNER DAD

Ah, the final frontier of Dad Jokedom: embracing your inner dad. This is where the grass is greener (because the lawn has been obsessively manicured), the puns are plentiful, and the BBQ grills are forever sizzling. If you've made it this far through this profound tome, then you're either fully committed to the art and science of Dad Joking, or you've lost your remote and are desperately looking for any form of entertainment. Either way, welcome to enlightenment, Dad Joke style.

Step One: Acceptance is the Key to Inner Peace (and Outer Groans)

The first step on the road to becoming a Dad Joke Guru is acceptance. Say it with me: "I have an inner dad, and that dad loves bad jokes." Go on, say it loud and proud. Done? No, your computer screen won't judge you. It's seen worse.

Step Two: Get the Gear

If you're going to look the part, you need the right apparel. Dig out those cargo shorts from the back of the closet. Find that cap you got as a promotional freebie from the hardware store. No, it doesn't matter if it advertises termite spray. The less context, the better. Don't forget those infamous dad sandals that pair splendidly with socks.

Step Three: Mastering the Dad Bod

DAD JOKES: WHY YOUR FAMILY IS AVOIDING YOU (CHUCKLE CHUMS)

Embracing your inner dad also involves embracing the dad bod. Now, don't get carried away; you don't have to dive headlong into a diet of pizza and beer. However, feel free to relax that six-pack into a more comfortable keg shape.

Step Four: Perfect the Dad Dance

You know the one. That awkward shuffle featuring random arm movements that vaguely resemble a dying bird attempting to take flight. The key to a successful Dad Dance is to be entirely unaware of its awkwardness. For full effect, break out this move during inappropriate times: PTA meetings, grocery store queues, or while waiting at the DMV.

Step Five: Become a Fact Machine

Any aspiring Dad Joke aficionado must also be a fount of utterly useless yet endlessly fascinating facts. Did you know that an octopus has three hearts? Or that you can't hum while holding your nose? No? Well, memorize these and other pointless tidbits to sprinkle throughout conversations like questionable seasoning on a casserole nobody asked for.

Step Six: Get the Language Down

Your vocabulary must undergo a dad-ification process. This means incorporating phrases like "Back in my day," "Let's rock and roll," and "Are we cooking with gas now?" into your daily dialogue. Extra points for using these expressions in settings where they make zero sense. For example, say, "Are we cooking with gas now?" while paying bills or cleaning the cat's litter box.

Step Seven: The Pun is Mightier than the Sword

The pun is the Excalibur of Dad Jokes, and you're the underqualified King Arthur. Whether it's "The chicken crossing the road" or "The bar you shouldn't walk into," wield your puns with the reckless abandon of a toddler holding a permanent marker. The world is your canvas; now go forth and pun-tificate.

Step Eight: Timing is Everything (Even When It's Nothing)

As you probably learned from previous chapters, timing in Dad Jokes is both a science and a wild, unchained art form, like interpretive dance or amateur taxidermy. The key to the timing of your jokes is unpredictability. Throw a Dad Joke into serious discussions about politics, investments, or the string theory. Your audience won't see it coming, much like a pigeon swooping in to steal a french fry.

Step Nine: Establish Your Signature Move

Every great superhero has a signature move, and so should you. Whether it's the dramatic pause, the exaggerated wink, or the self-congratulatory laugh that follows your joke, make it yours. Own it like you own that pristine lawn in your imaginary suburban kingdom.

Step Ten: Never, Ever, EVER Admit Defeat

You're going to tell bad jokes. Even worse than the usual Dad Joke standard. You'll hear crickets. You'll get blank stares. You may even get pelted with small vegetables. But remember, a true Dad Joke Maestro never admits defeat. Double down on the awkwardness. If your joke bombs, follow it up with another. And another. Like a comedy kamikaze, go down in a blaze of misguided humor.

The Ethical Responsibility of Embracing Your Inner Dad

Yes, yes, I know we already had a chapter on ethics, but this bears repeating. With great dad-ness comes great responsibility. Use your puns wisely. Understand your audience. And for heaven's sake, don't break out the Dad Jokes at somber events unless you're absolutely certain they'll land well—or you're just looking to never be invited again.

Conclusion: Becoming One with Your Inner Dad

If you follow these steps, your transformation into a full-fledged Dad Joke Jedi will be complete. You'll be the life of the party or, at the very least, the cause of its slow death. Either way, you'll be unforgettable.

So go forth, dear reader, armed with your puns, your dad bod, and your unyielding resolve. A world of groans awaits you—a symphony of sighs and eye rolls, each one a badge of honor in the dad-ly arts. May your jokes be terrible, your timing be worse, and your inner dad be as unshakable as that stain on your cargo shorts.

And thus, we conclude this comprehensive guide on Dad Jokes. It's been a ride filled with highs, lows, and middling plateaus of mild discomfort. Whether you're a dad, know a dad, or just love a good (or bad) joke, remember: The world may change, empires may rise and fall, but Dad Jokes are eternal. And for that, we owe our inner dads a hearty high-five and a cringe-worthy pun. After all, they've urned it. Get it? "Urn-ed"? Because it's a Dad Joke, and—oh, never mind.

Thank you, and goodnight. You've been a terrific audience. I'm here all week. Don't forget to tip your waiters.

CHAPTER 10: THE DAD JOKE MEDIATION: RECLAIMING YOUR FAMILY

Once upon a time, in a quaint suburban neighborhood, lived a man named Bob. Bob was your typical dad, complete with a dad bod and a penchant for dad jokes. He was a master of puns, a wizard of wordplay, and a connoisseur of groan-inducing humor. But there was one small problem: Bob's family had reached their breaking point. They were on the verge of abandoning ship, or in this case, the family dinner table.

It all began innocently enough. Bob's kids, Timmy and Jenny, used to adore his jokes. They'd giggle uncontrollably when he'd ask, "Why did the bicycle fall over? Because it was two-tired!" But as the years passed, those giggles turned into sighs and eye rolls. Timmy and Jenny began plotting ways to escape their dad's comedic clutches.

One fateful evening, as Bob was gearing up for yet another epic pun, Timmy whispered to Jenny, "We've got to do something about Dad's jokes. They're taking over our lives!" Jenny nodded in agreement, and thus, the idea for a dad joke intervention was born.

Section 1: Staging a Dad Joke Intervention: Step by Step

Fast forward to a sunny Saturday afternoon in the Johnson family living room. Timmy, Jenny, and their mom, Sarah, had gathered to discuss their plan. The family dog, Sparky, who had suffered through many a dad joke, also joined the meeting, wearing a look of canine concern.

Timmy, who had taken on the role of intervention coordinator, cleared his throat. "Okay, folks, it's time to take action. We can't let Dad's jokes destroy our family any longer."

Sarah, Bob's long-suffering wife, nodded. "I agree. I miss the days when we could have a conversation without a punchline."

Jenny chimed in, "And I miss being able to invite friends over without fearing Dad's jokes will embarrass me into oblivion."

With the Johnson family's grievances aired, Timmy proceeded to unveil the intervention plan.

Step 1: The Call to Action

Timmy explained, "The first step in reclaiming our family is realizing that Dad's jokes have gone too far. We're way past the point of no return."

Sarah added, "I mean, last week, I tried to have a serious discussion about our finances, and he responded with, 'Why did the scarecrow win an award? Because he was outstanding in his field!' It's a problem."

Step 2: Assembling the Intervention Team

The next item on the agenda was assembling the intervention team. Timmy emphasized, "We need allies who share our family's best interests, which likely involves fewer puns. We should invite Aunt Linda and Uncle Mark. They've always been on our side when it comes to Dad's jokes."

Sarah nodded in agreement, "That's true, and they've managed to have a normal conversation with Bob on occasion."

Jenny, the family diplomat, added, "Let's make sure to avoid inviting Grandpa Joe, though. He's part of the problem. I've heard him and Dad share dad jokes like it's a secret handshake."

Step 3: Setting the Stage

On the day of the intervention, the living room was chosen as the neutral location for the proceedings. It was selected for its lack of pun-related decorations and because it had plain walls that wouldn't distract from the seriousness of the intervention.

The family dog, Sparky, was given the important task of guarding the door to ensure Bob didn't escape prematurely. Sparky, though a loyal companion, had mixed feelings about this responsibility. He'd seen his fair share of dad jokes, and they often left him feeling existentially confused.

Step 4: The "Dad Joke-ervention" Banner

Timmy, the mastermind behind the operation, hung up a banner that read, "Dad Joke-ervention Zone." The banner was equal parts festive and foreboding, sending a clear message that this was not a time for humor.

Jenny couldn't help but chuckle at the banner. "I have to admit, this is kinda funny, even if it's at Dad's expense."

Timmy grinned, "Well, a little humor can't hurt as long as it's not a dad joke."

Step 5: The Groan-O-Meter

To provide empirical evidence of Bob's dad joke impact, Timmy installed a Groan-O-Meter on the wall. It was a simple device with a scale ranging from "Mild Chuckle" to "Epic Eye Roll" to "Audible Groan." Family members could rate the intensity of their reactions to Bob's jokes throughout the intervention.

Sparky, who had been observing the Groan-O-Meter installation with great interest, woofed in agreement. It seemed even the dog was on board with the intervention plan.

With all preparations in place, the Johnson family anxiously awaited the arrival of their dad and the impending showdown of puns versus reason.

Section 2: When All Else Fails - Join the Dad Joke Support Group

Sometimes, even the most well-intentioned interventions fail. If your family remains unconvinced that you need to ease up on the puns, it might be time to seek help from those who truly understand your struggle – the Dad Joke Support Group.

Step 1: Finding the Support Group

Bob Johnson, our pun-loving protagonist, was completely unaware of his family's intervention plans. Little did he know that there was a secret underground network of dad joke enthusiasts who met in basements, community centers, and online forums. This network was known as the Dad Joke Support Group, and it was about to change Bob's life.

One evening, as Bob was browsing the internet in search of new puns, he stumbled upon an online forum called "Dad Joke Enthusiasts Unite!" Intrigued, he clicked on the link and was greeted by a digital treasure trove of puns, jokes, and fellow dads who reveled in wordplay.

Bob read through the forum posts, chuckling at each witty retort and clever one-liner. It was a digital haven for dad joke aficionados, a place where puns flowed like a never-ending stream.

Step 2: Group Therapy

As Bob immersed himself in the world of the Dad Joke Support Group, he couldn't help but feel a sense of belonging. These were his people, individuals who understood the joy of a well-timed pun and the agony of a perfectly good dad joke going unappreciated.

One evening, Bob decided to share his own dad joke story on the forum. He wrote about the time he had tried to lighten the mood at a family gathering with a pun about cheese, only to be met with a chorus of groans. He described the disappointment he felt and how he had been on the verge of giving up his beloved dad jokes.

To his surprise, the forum members responded with empathy and support. They shared their own experiences of pun rejection and offered words of encouragement. It was a cathartic experience for Bob, a moment of shared vulnerability with fellow pun enthusiasts.

Step 3: Gradual Withdrawal

As Bob continued to engage with the Dad Joke Support Group, he began to realize that there was more to life than puns. He learned that moderation was key and that there was a time and place for dad jokes.

The support group guided him through a gradual withdrawal process from dad jokes. They encouraged him to replace puns with compliments and genuine conversation topics. Bob started to ask his family about their day, their interests, and their dreams, instead of launching into pun-filled anecdotes.

At first, it felt strange to Bob, like he was navigating uncharted territory. But as he witnessed the positive impact of his newfound approach on his family, he began to see the value in connecting on a deeper level.

Step 4: Celebrating Milestones

The Dad Joke Support Group celebrated Bob's dad joke-free achievements with non-pun-related parties. These gatherings were filled with laughter, camaraderie, and a surprising absence of groans. Bob discovered that life without constant wordplay could actually be enjoyable.

During one such celebration, Bob was awarded the "Most Improved Conversationalist" trophy. It was a far cry from his previous "Dad Joke Champion" title, but he wore it with pride.

As Bob continued his journey of self-improvement, he found himself not only reconnecting with his family but also rediscovering the joy of genuine laughter and meaningful conversations. He realized that he could still inject humor into his interactions without resorting to puns and that there was more to him than just his dad joke persona.

Conclusion: The Dad Joke Intervention – A Success Story

In the end, the Johnson family's intervention proved successful. Bob, with the support of the Dad Joke Support Group, had transformed from a pun-spewing machine into a more balanced and thoughtful conversationalist.

The Groan-O-Meter, once a constant presence in the Johnson family home, had been retired to the attic, a relic of the past. Instead, the living room now echoed with genuine laughter and engaging conversations.

The family dog, Sparky, wore a contented expression as he lounged on the carpet, no longer subjected to existential canine dilemmas triggered by dad jokes.

And so, dear reader, the story of Bob and his dad joke intervention serves as a testament to the power of family, support, and the ability to change for the better. It's a tale of redemption, laughter, and the enduring quest to find humor in the everyday moments of life, without resorting to the dreaded pun.

CHAPTER 11: FROM GROANS TO GRINS: REDEMPTION STORIES

Bob Johnson, once the unrelenting punster of the Johnson family, had undergone a dramatic transformation. With the guidance of the Dad Joke Support Group, he had learned to temper his pun addiction, embracing a life filled with genuine laughter and meaningful conversations. But what about other dad joke enthusiasts who found themselves in the same punny predicament? Let's explore some redemption stories that will have you going from groans to grins.

Redemption Story 1: The Office Joker's Turnaround

In the heart of the business district stood the towering skyscraper that housed Bland & Boring Inc., a company known for its, well, blandness. At the center of this corporate hive was Gary, the notorious office joker.

Gary had a penchant for interrupting board meetings with puns and turning coffee breaks into stand-up comedy sessions. His coworkers would groan, sigh, and sometimes consider jumping out of the nearest window to escape his relentless humor. But Gary was blissfully unaware of their suffering, or he just didn't care.

One day, Gary received an anonymous email inviting him to a top-secret meeting. The subject line read, "Dad Joke Support Group - Your Last Hope."

Curiosity piqued, Gary followed the email's instructions and found himself in a dimly lit room filled with fellow pun enthusiasts, all with similar stories of groaning coworkers and exasperated bosses.

As the group shared their experiences, Gary realized that his addiction to puns had consequences far beyond a few eye rolls. His coworkers were on the brink of staging an intervention, and his boss had threatened to send him to a "Dad Joke Rehabilitation Center."

Determined to change, Gary made a vow to his fellow group members that he would tone down his pun game at the office. He even went as far as to attend a stand-up comedy workshop to channel his humor in more appropriate ways.

Weeks turned into months, and slowly but surely, Gary transformed from the office joker to the office funny guy. His colleagues began looking forward to his humor, and he found that he could still make people laugh without resorting to groan-inducing puns.

At the annual office party, Gary gave a heartfelt speech about his journey from groans to grins. He thanked his coworkers for their patience and promised to keep the puns to a minimum. The room erupted in applause, and for the first time in years, Gary was the life of the party without causing any eye rolls.

Redemption Story 2: Dad Joke Saves a Marriage

Bob Johnson wasn't the only dad who had faced a dad joke intervention. Meet Steve, a dedicated dad who had a knack for puns that could rival Bob's. Steve's wife, Lisa, had reached her breaking point.

Every evening, as they sat down for dinner, Steve would unleash a barrage of dad jokes. Lisa, once enamored by his humor, now dreaded mealtime. She couldn't take it anymore, and she knew that something had to change.

One day, while scrolling through social media, Lisa stumbled upon an article about the "Dad Joke Support Group" and the remarkable transformation of Bob Johnson. Intrigued, she decided to do some research and found the contact information for the group.

After a tense family dinner that left everyone groaning, Lisa approached Steve with a proposal. "Steve, I love you, but I can't handle the dad jokes anymore. If we don't do something about this, I'm afraid it will tear us apart."

Steve, surprised and concerned by Lisa's sincerity, agreed to give the Dad Joke Support Group a try. The next week, they attended their first meeting together.

As they listened to other families share their stories, Steve and Lisa realized that they weren't alone in their struggle. They saw the potential for dad jokes to bring joy rather than annoyance. Steve decided to undergo the same transformation that Bob had experienced.

With the support of the group, Steve gradually reduced the frequency of his puns at home. He focused on making Lisa laugh in other ways, surprising her with sweet gestures and thoughtful conversations. It wasn't long before their dinner table transformed from a groan zone to a place of genuine connection and shared laughter.

One evening, as they enjoyed a quiet dinner together, Steve couldn't resist a well-timed pun. Lisa chuckled, genuinely amused, and Steve felt a rush of satisfaction. He had found the balance between being a loving husband and a dad with a sense of humor.

Their marriage grew stronger as they rediscovered the joy of each other's company. Steve and Lisa even started attending comedy shows together, relishing the laughter they shared without the need for groans.

Redemption Story 3: A Dad Joke Charity Gala

Across town, in the bustling community of Oakville, another dad named Tom had a similar transformation. Tom was known for his dad jokes that ranged from clever wordplay to painfully punny. His children, Emma and Ethan, had grown up with their dad's humor and were used to the eye rolls and groans it elicited.

One day, while Emma was browsing the internet for a school project on charity events, she stumbled upon the "Dad Joke Charity Gala." It was an event that celebrated dad jokes while raising funds for a good cause. Emma couldn't help but think that this could be the perfect way to channel her dad's pun-loving energy for a greater purpose.

Excited, she approached her dad with the idea of participating in the gala. Tom, always up for a new pun-related adventure, agreed without hesitation. Together, they started brainstorming their act.

For weeks, Tom and Emma practiced their routine, crafting puns that were witty and groan-worthy in equal measure. They rehearsed in secret, not wanting to reveal their performance until the night of the gala.

The evening of the Dad Joke Charity Gala arrived, and the Oakville community gathered in anticipation. Tom and Emma took the stage, and the room was filled with a sense of curiosity and amusement.

Their routine was a whirlwind of puns, wordplay, and dad jokes that had the audience laughing and groaning in equal measure. Tom and Emma's chemistry on stage was undeniable, and their act became a highlight of the evening.

But the best part was yet to come. At the end of their performance,

Tom and Emma revealed their true purpose. They explained that all the proceeds from their act, as well as the entire gala, would be donated to a local charity that supported underprivileged children.

The audience was moved by their generosity, and a wave of applause and cheers filled the room. Tom, once known for his groan-inducing puns, had become a local hero, using his humor for a meaningful cause.

Conclusion: The Transformation of Dad Joke Enthusiasts

The redemption stories of Gary, Steve, and Tom serve as a testament to the power of change and the possibility of growth, even for the most enthusiastic dad joke enthusiasts. Through self-awareness, support, and a willingness to adapt, these dads turned their groans into grins and transformed their relationships and communities in the process.

As Bob Johnson, Steve, Tom, and countless others have shown, dad jokes can be a force for good when used in moderation and with consideration for those around us. So, the next time you find yourself caught in the crossfire of a dad joke onslaught, remember that there's hope for a groan-free future, filled with genuine laughter and meaningful connections.

APPENDIX: 200 DAD JOKES

Congratulations! You've made it to the appendix, the caboose of this literary train, where we present to you a treasure trove of Dad Jokes for every occasion. Use them wisely, use them freely, and above all, use them responsibly. Each of these jokes has been carefully selected to ensure maximum groan potential while remaining family-friendly and appropriate for all audiences. So without further ado, let's dig into this comedic goldmine!

Classic Dad Jokes

1. Why did the scarecrow win an award?
- Because he was outstanding in his field!

2. How do you organize a space party?
- You "planet."

3. What do you call fake spaghetti?
- An "impasta."

4. How does a penguin build its house?
- Igloos it together.

5. Why don't scientists trust atoms?

- Because they make up everything!

Animal-Themed Dad Jokes

6. Why did the duck get kicked out of the pond?
- Because he kept quacking up all the other ducks.

7. How do you catch a squirrel?
- Climb a tree and act like a nut!

8. What do you call an alligator in a vest?
- An "investigator."

9. Why did the cow sit down at the table?
- It saw the steaks were high.

10. What do you call a pile of cats?
- A "meow-tain."

Food-Themed Dad Jokes

11. What do you call cheese that isn't yours?
- Nacho cheese!

12. Why did the tomato turn red?
- Because it saw the salad dressing.

13. How do you make a lemon drop?
- Just let it fall.

14. What did the grape say when it got stepped on?
- Nothing, it just let out a little "wine."

15. Why did the bread file a complaint?
- It kept getting "torn apart."

Tech-Themed Dad Jokes

16. Why did the computer go to the doctor?
- It had too many viruses.

17. How do you comfort a JavaScript bug?
- You "console" it!

18. Why do programmers prefer dark mode?
- Because light attracts bugs!

19. How many programmers does it take to change a light bulb?
- None. That's a hardware problem.

20. Why did the computer take up gardening?
- Because it wanted to improve its "root" access.

Dad Jokes for Every Season

21. What do you call an arrogant snowman?
- "Snow-it-all."

22. Why did summer catch autumn?
- Because autumn kept "falling."

23. What did the tree say to spring?
- "What a re-leaf."

24. How did winter say goodbye to fall?
- "I'll catch you next year when you drop!"

25. Why did summer break up with spring?
- It needed "space."

The Pinnacle of Dad Jokery

26. What did one hat say to the other hat?
- "You stay here. I'll go on ahead."

27. How do you make a tissue dance?
- You put a little "boogie" in it!

28. Why did the bicycle fall over?
- Because it was "two-tired."

29. Why did the math book look sad?
- Because it had too many "problems."

Wordplay Dad Jokes

31. What do you call someone who steals energy?
- A "joule thief."

32. What's the best tool to do math?
- "Multi-pliers."

33. Why did the golfer bring two pairs of pants?
- In case he got a hole in one.

34. What did one wall say to the other?
- "I'll meet you at the corner."

35. What did the stamp say to the envelope?
- "Stick with me, and we'll go places!"

Everyday Dad Jokes

36. Why did the teddy bear say "No" to dessert?
- Because he was already "stuffed."

37. Why did the man put his money in the blender?
- Because he wanted to make "liquid assets."

38. How do you catch a unique animal?
- "Unique" up on it!

39. Why did the calendar go to the doctor?
- Because it's days were numbered.

Musical Dad Jokes

41. Why did the music teacher go to jail?
- Because she got caught with too many "sharp objects."

42. What's a composer's favorite snack?
- "Chopin"-olate.

43. Why did the musician break up with the metronome?
- Because it couldn't keep up!

44. What's Beethoven's favorite fruit?
- "Ba-na-na-na."

45. How do you fix a broken tuba?
- With a "tuba glue."

Sports Dad Jokes

46. Why did the fish refuse to play basketball?
- It was afraid of the net.

47. Why did the football team go to the bakery?
- To get a better "batter."

48. What did the baseball glove say to the ball?
- "Catch you later!"

49. Why did the basketball player go to therapy?

- He had "hoop issues."

50. How do soccer players stay cool during games?
- They stand near the "fans."

Dad Jokes of the Future

51. Why did the robot go on a diet?
- It had too many "bytes."

52. What do you call a belt with a watch on it?
- A "waist of time."

53. Why did the smartphone go to therapy?
- It lost its "sync."

54. How do you stop an astronaut's baby from crying?
- You "rocket."

55. What did the digital clock say to its mom?
- "Look, Ma! No hands!"

Ultimate Dad Jokes

56. Why did the football team go to the bank?
- To get their quarterback.

57. What's brown and sticky?
- A stick.

58. Why did the belt get arrested?
- Because it was holding up a pair of pants.

59. Why did the scarecrow break up with the cornstalk?
- He thought it was too "ear-responsible."

60. What did one ocean say to the other ocean?
- Nothing, it just "waved."

Geography Dad Jokes

61. What did Delaware?
- A "New Jersey."

62. What's the capital of Alaska?
- "Come on, Juneau this one!"

63. What's a city's favorite type of music?
- "Urban."

64. What did one tectonic plate say to the other?
- "You crack me up!"

65. How do you get from here to Antarctica?
- "I don't know, I've never "polar" there!"

Automotive Dad Jokes

66. Why did the car apply for a job?
- It wanted to quit being a "junker."

67. What type of car does a Jedi drive?
- A "Toy-Yoda."

68. What did the traffic light say to the car?
- "Don't look, I'm changing."

69. Why don't cars ever get tired?
- Because they always "come with a spare."

70. What's a car's favorite meal?
- "Brake-fast."

Health & Wellness Dad Jokes

71. Why did the pilates instructor get fired?
- Because she was always "bent out of shape."

72. Why did the dumbbell break up with the treadmill?
- It felt "walked on."

73. What did one plate say to another?
- "Tonight, dinner's on me."

74. Why didn't the dad tell a joke about pizza?
- Because it's too cheesy.

75. What did the femur say to the patella?
- "I kneed you."

Fashion Dad Jokes

76. What did the hat say to the scarf?
- "You hang around, I'll go on ahead."

77. Why did the belt get promoted?
- Because it really held things together.

78. What's a shoe's favorite type of chips?
- "Lace."

79. Why did the shirt get kicked out of school?
- Because it was always "tearing up."

80. What did one shoe say to the other?
- "You're my sole mate."

Education Dad Jokes

81. What did the history book say to the geography book?
- "You've got a lot of territory to cover."

82. What did the triangle say to the circle?
- "You're so pointless."

83. What's a teacher's favorite nation?
- "Expla-nation."

84. Why did the physics book break up with the math book?
- It found it too "formulaic."

85. What did the biology textbook say to the physics textbook?
- "You matter, but I've got more "organs."

Outdoor Dad Jokes

86. What's a tree's least favorite month?
- Sep-"timber!"

87. What did the vegetable wear to the pool party?
- A zucchini.

88. How do you make a flower bed?
- With sheets, pillows, and planty of room.

89. Why did the tomato turn red?
- Because it saw the "salad dressing."

90. Why did the tree get into trouble?
- Because it was always "going out on a limb."

DIY Dad Jokes

91. Why did the wood file a complaint against the hammer?

- Because it was always getting "nailed."

92. How many carpenters does it take to change a light bulb?
- None. That's a job for the electricians!

93. Why did the dad buy a new ladder?
- Because he thought it would elevate his work.

94. Why did the builder break up with the decorator?
- There were too many walls between them.

95. Why did the tape measure get frustrated?
- Because it could never "measure up."

Historical Dad Jokes

96. Why did the scarecrow become a successful banker?
- Because he was great at "straw investing."

97. What was King Arthur's favorite game?
- "Knights and crosses."

98. What a historians favorite dessert?
- "Past-ries."

99. Why did Cleopatra break up with the Pharaoh?
- He was in de-Nile about his faults.

100. What's Julius Caesar's favorite salad?
- "Caesar salad," of course!

Workplace Dad Jokes

101. Why did the warden send the prisoners to a spreadsheet?
- It had plenty of cells.

102.   Why did the office chair get promoted?
•   Because it always had its employees' back.

103.   Why did the businessman read a self-help book?
•   He wanted to get to the "bottom line."

104.   Why did the broken pencil get kicked out of the meeting?
•   Because it was always "pointless."

105.   What do you call a parade of office workers?
•   A "bored-walk."

Weather Dad Jokes

106.   Why did the cloud get kicked out of the group?
•   Because it was too "dark."

107.   What do you call dangerous precipitation?
•   A "rain of terror."

108.   Why did the weather reporter get kicked off the air?
•   For "foggy" reporting.

109.   Why did the sun take a break?
•   It needed to "lighten up."

110.   What's a tornado's favorite game?
•   "Twister."

Holiday Dad Jokes

111.   Why did the Easter Egg hide?
•   It was a little "chicken."

112.   What do you call Santa when he loses his pants?
•   "Saint Knickerless."

113.   Why did the turkey join a band?
- Because it had the "drumsticks."

114.   Whats a snowmans favorite dish?
- "Brrr-itos."

115.   What did the pumpkin say to the pumpkin carver?
- "Cut it out."

Artistic Dad Jokes

116.   What did one sketchbook say to the other?
- "I think you're drawing too much attention."

117.   Why did the artist get kicked out of the museum?
- Because he was too "sketchy."

118.   What did the paint say to the canvas?
- "I've got you covered."

119.   Why was the painter always calm?
- Because he knew how to brush things off.

120.   Why did the artist go to jail?
- He was caught framing someone.

Philosophical Dad Jokes

121.   What did Descartes say when he was offered dessert?
- "I think, therefore I flan."

122.   Why did the chicken have an existential crisis?
- It couldn't figure out the meaning of crossing the road.

123.   What's a philosopher's favorite beverage?

- "Socratea."

124.　What did the pessimist philosopher order at the bar?
- A glass half empty.

125.　Why don't philosophers play chess?
- They are always in check with reality.

Legal Dad Jokes

126.　What's a lawyers favorite hobby?
- Lien on people.

127.　What did the lawyer name his daughter?
- "Sue."

128.　Why did the lawyer get thrown out of the restaurant?
- He wanted to "pass the bar."

129.　Why did the lawyer bring a pencil to court?
- To draw his own conclusions.

130.　Whats a lawyers favorite snack?
- "Sue-shi."

Foodie Dad Jokes

131.　Why did the cucumber seek counseling?
- It couldn't get itself out of a "pickle."

132.　What's a potato's favorite horror movie?
- "The Silence of the Yams."

133.　What's a pancakes job in baseball?
- The batter.

134. Why did the yogurt go to art school?
- It wanted to get cultured.

135. Why did the orange lose the race?
- It ran out of juice.

Relationship Dad Jokes

136. Why did the phone wear glasses?
- It lost all its "contacts."

137. What did one boat say to the other boat?
- "Are you up for a little row-mance?"

138. What did the zero say to the eight?
- "Nice belt!"

139. Why did the girl bring a ladder to her date?
- She heard she was going out with a "tall drink of water."

140. How did the smartphone propose?
- With a ring-tone.

Social Media Dad Jokes

141. Why did Twitter file a complaint?
- It was tired of being "followed."

142. Why did the Snapchat message get in trouble at school?
- Because it couldn't stay for the whole class.

143. Why did the musician hate social media?
- Because he couldn't find the right "key" for likes.

144. How does a social media manager flirt?
- "Are you a Wi-Fi signal? Because I'm really feeling a

connection."

145.   Why did Instagram go to art school?
• To learn more "filters."

Exercise and Gym Dad Jokes

146.   How did the dad quit being a personal trainer?
• But then he gave his too weak notice.

147.   What's a gym's favorite type of music?
• Heavy Metal

148.   What's a weightlifter's favorite game?
• "Set-lers of Catan."

149.   Why did the gym close early?
• It wasn't "working out."

150.   What did the gym shorts say to the sneakers?
• "Shoe, you stink."

Pet Dad Jokes

151.   Why did the cat sit next to the computer?
• To keep an eye on the mouse.

152.   What did one flea say to the other?
• "Should we walk or take a dog?"

153.   Why do you call a snake that bakes?
• "A Pie-thon."

154.   What do you call a pony with a sore throat?
• "A little hoarse."

155.   What's a goldfish's favorite story?
· Anything that has a good hook.

Financial Dad Jokes

156.   Why are piggybanks so wise?
· Because they are filled with common sense.

157.   What's a hedge fund manager's favorite type of music?
· "Heavy Metal," because they love to "rock the market."

158.   Why did the credit card get therapy?
· It was fed up with the constant "charges" against it.

159.   What did the one-dollar bill say to the twenty-dollar bill?
· "You're so full of yourself, always acting like you're the change everyone wants to see in the world."

160.   Why did the stock get thrown out of the party?
· It was too "volatile," always dipping and soaring.

Adventure and Outdoor Dad Jokes

161.   Why did the camping trip get canceled?
· It was just too "in-tents."

162.   How can you tell if a tree is a dogwood tree?
· By its bark.

163.   Which states has the most streets?
· Road-Island.

164.   What did the mountain say to the mountaineer?
· "You take me for 'granite.'"

165.   Why couldn't the dad catch the fog?

- He kept misting.

Home Improvement Dad Jokes

166. How did the nail greet the hammer?
- "Hit me up sometime!"

167. Why didn't the construction worker tell his joke?
- Because he was still working on it.

168. Why did the light bulb fail its exam?
- Because it wasn't that "bright."

169. What did the HVAC say to the homeowner?
- "I'm your biggest fan!"

170. Why did the rug complain?
- Because people kept "walking all over it."

Too Punny Dad Jokes

171. Why can't a nose be 12 inches long?
- Because then it would be a foot.

172. What do you call someone with no body and no nose?
- "Nobody knows."

173. What did the dad say when asked if he got a hair cut?
- "No, I got them all cut."

174. What did the janitor say when he jumped out of the closet?
- "Supplies!"

175. Why did the hot air balloon get a promotion?
- It was really "rising" in the company.

Technology Dad Jokes

176.   What's a robots favorite snack?
· Computer chips.

177.   What did the laptop say to the desktop?
· "You're so 'towering' over me."

178.   Why did the smartphone go to therapy?
· It lost its "sense of touch."

179.   What did the Wi-Fi say to the router?
· "We have a 'connection.'"

180.   Why did the software developer go broke?
· He kept using up all his "cache."

Most Ridiculous Dad Jokes

181.   What time did the dad go to the dentist?
· Tooth-hurty.

182.   How do you make 7 even?
· Take away the 'S.'

183.   How many tickles does it take to make an octopus laught?
· Ten-tickles.

184.   What kind of car does an egg drive?
· "A Yolkswagon."

185.   What kind of shoes do ninjas wear?
· Sneakers.

Celestial Dad Jokes

186.   Why did the sun graduate college early?
· Because it was so "bright."

187.   What did Earth say to Mars?
· "You have no life!"

188.   Why did the moon file for bankruptcy?
· It was "out of its phase."

189.   What did the star say to the galaxy?
· "You make my world go round."

190.   Why did the comet get kicked out of the Solar System?
· It was always "streaking."

Seasonal Dad Jokes

191.   Why did Winter break up with Summer?
· Because Summer was too "hot" to handle.

192.   Why did Winter admire Autumn?
· It was always so cool.

193.   What do you call a snowman with a tan?
· A puddle.

194.   What did Autumn say to its leaves?
· "You're falling for me."

195.   Can February March?
· No but April May.

Marine Life Dad Jokes

196.   Why did the shark blush?
· It saw the ocean's bottom.

197.   What did one fish say to the other?
- "Keep your mouth closed, or you'll be on the hook!"

198.   Why did the crab never give to charity?
- Because he was shellfish.

199.   How do clams call their friends?
- On their "shell phones."

200.   Why did the octopus cross the coral reef?
- To get to the other tide.

Made in the USA
Middletown, DE
22 October 2023

41232384R00044